CAREERS ON THE FRONT LINE

UNDERCOVER OPERATIONS CAREERS

HEATHER C. HUDAK

CRABTREE
PUBLISHING COMPANY
WWW.CRABTREEBOOKS.COM

CRABTREE
PUBLISHING COMPANY
WWW.CRABTREEBOOKS.COM

Author: Heather C. Hudak
Editors: Sarah Eason
   Jennifer Sanderson
   Ellen Rodger
Proofreader: Tracey Kelly
Indexer: Tracey Kelly
Editorial director:
   Kathy Middleton
Interior design: Emma DeBanks
Cover and logo design:
   Katherine Berti
Photo research: Rachel Blount
Print coordinator:
   Katherine Berti
Consultant: David Hawksett

Written, developed, and produced for Crabtree
   Publishing by Calcium Creative Ltd.

Photo Credits:
t=Top, tr=Top Right, tl=Top Left
Inside: Shutterstock: ASDF_MEDIA:
p. 9; Couperfield: pp. 1, 27; Michael
Fitzsimmons: pp. 18–19; Gorodenkoff:
pp. 3, 5, 8, 28b, 29; Matej Kastelic:
p. 23; Dmitri Ma: p. 28t; Monkey
Business Images: p. 21; NDAB
Creativity: p. 25; Photographee.eu: p.
7, 20; The Rabbit Hole: p. 4; Maksim
Shmeljov: p. 13; Syda Productions: p.
6; Wavebreakmedia: p. 24; U.S. Army:
Staff Sgt. Matt Britton: p. 17; Wikimedia
Commons: FBI: p. 12; IIP Photo
Archive: p. 11; Aaron Tang: p. 15; U.S.
Navy photo by Mass Communication
Specialist 2nd Class Martin L. Carey: p.
16. Front cover: Shutterstock

Library and Archives Canada Cataloguing in Publication

Title: Careers in undercover operations / Heather C. Hudak.
Names: Hudak, Heather C., 1975- author.
Description: Series statement: Careers on the front line |
   Includes bibliographical references and index.
Identifiers: Canadiana (print) 20200283871 |
   Canadiana (ebook) 2020028388X |
   ISBN 9780778781394 (hardcover) |
   ISBN 9780778781455 (softcover) |
   ISBN 9781427125798 (HTML)
Subjects: LCSH: Undercover operations—United States—
   Juvenile literature. | LCSH: Undercover operations—
   Canada—Juvenile literature. | LCSH: Intelligence service—
   Vocational guidance—United States—Juvenile literature. |
LCSH: Intelligence service—Vocational guidance—Canada—
   Juvenile literature.
Classification: LCC HV8080.U5 H83 2020 | DDC j363.2/32—dc23

Library of Congress Cataloging-in-Publication Data
Names: Hudak, Heather C., 1975- author.
Title: Careers in undercover operations / Heather C. Hudak.
Description: New York : Crabtree Publishing Company, [2021]
   | Series: Careers on the front line | Includes index.
Identifiers: LCCN 2020029747 (print) |
   LCCN 2020029748 (ebook) |
   ISBN 9780778781394 (hardcover) |
   ISBN 9780778781455 (paperback) |
   ISBN 9781427125798 (ebook)
Subjects: LCSH: Undercover operations--Vocational guidance-
   -Juvenile literature. | United States. Federal Bureau of Investigation.
Classification: LCC HV8080.U5 H83 2021 (print) |
   LCC HV8080.U5 (ebook) | DDC 363.2/32--dc23
LC record available at https://lccn.loc.gov/2020029747
LC ebook record available at https://lccn.loc.gov/2020029748

Crabtree Publishing Company
www.crabtreebooks.com   1-800-387-7650

Printed in the U.S.A./082020/CG20200710

Copyright © **2021 CRABTREE PUBLISHING COMPANY**. All rights reserved. No part of this publication may be reproduced, stored in a retrieval system, or be transmitted in any form or by any means, electronic, mechanical, photocopying, recording, or otherwise, without the prior written permission of Crabtree Publishing Company. In Canada: We acknowledge the financial support of the Government of Canada through the Canada Book Fund for our publishing activities.

Published in Canada
Crabtree Publishing
616 Welland Ave.
St. Catharines, Ontario
L2M 5V6

Published in the United States
Crabtree Publishing
347 Fifth Ave
Suite 1402-145
New York, NY 10016

Published in the United Kingdom
Crabtree Publishing
Maritime House
Basin Road North, Hove
BN41 1WR

Published in Australia
Crabtree Publishing
3 Charles Street
Coburg North
VIC, 3058

CONTENTS

Secret Defense 4

Frontline Lives..6

The CIA 8

CIA Stories The Canadian Six: MOVIE MAGIC 10

The FBI..12

FBI Stories Tamer Elnoury: TERROR PLOT RUINED..............14

U.S. Special Operations Forces...16

Operation Stories Delta Force: FIGHTING ISIS 18

Police Force..20

Police Stories Mr. Big: CAPTURING A SUSPECT 22

Missions Behind the Front Line 24

Support Stories Monique Brillhart: FBI FORENSICS..............26

Could You Be on the Front Line?...28

Glossary 30

Learning More...31

Index and About the Author 32

SECRET DEFENSE

Undercover operations are all about **investigation**. **Law enforcement agencies**, such as the police, military, and **secret service agencies**, often run undercover investigations so they can watch criminals and gather information without them knowing about it. Undercover agents, or officers, are the people who do this kind of work. They collect **evidence** and information that can be used to convict criminals and keep the public safe.

SECRET AGENTS

Most undercover agents pretend to be someone other than whom they really are. They try to blend in with the people around them so that no one knows what they really do for a living. This protects them from being discovered as a member of a law enforcement agency. It also allows them to gain the trust of the people they investigate. The agent's goal is to get people to share information that can help solve or prevent crimes. Some agents do not play a role. University professors, scientists, computer programmers, and other experts are hired to secretly gather information while doing their regular jobs. They speak with other experts or people in their industry and report back to the agency that hired them.

Undercover agents change the way they look and dress to blend in with the people they are investigating.

4

Undercover agents work to track down hackers. Hackers are criminals who try to access computer systems.

MAFIA MAN

Some undercover agents work to prevent **terrorist** attacks or solve crimes that involve computers, known as cybercrimes. Others investigate **organized crime rings** or drug dealers. Jack Garcia is said to be the most successful undercover agent in the history of the FBI. He is most famous for helping to bring down top members of the Gambino family of New York. Some of the Gambino family ran an organized crime ring. Trainers from the **Federal Bureau of Investigation (FBI)** taught Garcia how to dress, talk, and act like a mobster, so that he could fit in with the Gambinos. Then, he pretended to be a jewel thief and drug dealer. He spent three years undercover working as a mobster.

Your FRONTLINE Career

Look for "Your Frontline Career" boxes. They highlight the skills and strengths needed for specific undercover careers. They can be used to help you decide whether a career as an undercover agent is for you and what roles might suit you best.

FRONTLINE LIVES

Undercover work is dangerous. Some agents risk getting killed. Some working in other countries risk prison. For this reason, their work is highly confidential, or secret. They tell only those people who are part of the investigation about the work they do. Most agents do not even tell their families about their jobs. Agents may not have any contact with friends or family during an investigation. This helps keep them from blowing their **cover**. It also protects their families from getting in the middle of high-risk situations.

HARD WORK

Agents often work long hours, even during evenings and weekends. They may need to take part in illegal activities to gain trust and fit in with the people they are investigating. Most undercover agents do not wear uniforms or carry any evidence that they are agents, such as a badge. They wear plain clothes so they do not stand out. They carry a gun only if their role calls for it. It can be hard for agents to return to their normal life after the operation is over. Some need counseling to help them adjust.

Agents may pose as drug dealers or other kinds of criminals, so they can become part of a crime ring.

AGENTS IN ACTION

It is very common for law enforcement agencies to send undercover agents to conferences around the world. Sometimes, they work as spies to gather top secret information for the U.S. government. Other times, they try to recruit scientists and industry experts from other countries. The plan is to bring these specialists' knowledge to the United States or to keep them from using their intelligence to aid the governments in their countries.

Undercover agents may only commit a crime if their cover will be blown if they do not do it.

MISTAKEN IDENTITY

Most undercover agents work far from home to avoid being recognized by friends or family. Sometimes, undercover agents are mistaken as suspects. They are so good at blending in that they seem like real criminals. They may be arrested or held at gunpoint by police officers who do not know their real **identity**. Agents are taught to keep still in such situations. They are trained not to reach for their gun or badge and to just do as the officer says.

THE CIA

The **Central Intelligence Agency (CIA)** is responsible for collecting and analyzing information from other countries about national **security threats**. The CIA investigates foreign governments, industries, military units, and terrorist groups. Sometimes, the CIA uses spies who are undercover to gather information. The president and other government leaders use the information provided by spies to guide their decisions and actions.

SECRET SERVICE

Only a select group of CIA agents work undercover. They are part of the Directorate of Operations, or **National Clandestine Service (NCS)**. There are two types of agents who work in this branch of the CIA: core collectors and operations officers. Core collectors look for sources of information, such as documents or **informants** who have access to details about a security threat. Operations officers then try to get the informant to share any details with them. Most agents in an official undercover role work overseas. They pose as employees of other U.S. government agencies.

Some CIA agents perform electronic surveillance. They might monitor a suspect's emails, Internet searches, and computer databases.

About 30 percent of the CIA's 20,000 employees have worked undercover at some point.

CANADIAN SPIES

The Canadian Security Intelligence Service (CSIS) is Canada's version of the CIA. It investigates activities that are seen as a threat to Canada's security. CSIS gets information from foreign and local governments, police forces, and informants. It also uses spies to conduct undercover operations. It then informs the government of Canada about possible threats, so that the government can take measures to stop them.

SPECIAL SKILLS

The CIA needs experts in all fields, but finance, **nuclear** science, and international business are of special interest. Many agents speak more than one language and are encouraged to learn others. Most undercover agents are well educated and have several years of experience working in the military or for a business. They travel the world and spend time working with people from many **cultures**. Agents must be able to handle high levels of stress and quickly adapt to any situation. They must have a good understanding of foreign affairs and be very good at meeting new people. They have to be able to form lasting relationships with informants who can provide them with top secret information.

CIA Stories

The Canadian Six:

MOVIE MAGIC

Ayatollah Khomeini was a professor in Iran in the mid-1900s. In 1964, he was **exiled**, for speaking out against the ruler of Iran, known as the Shah. Khomeini said the Shah should be overthrown. From exile, Khomeini organized an uprising against the Shah. In January 1978, protesters took a stand against the government as part of the Iranian Revolution. On January 16, 1979, the Shah fled to Egypt. Two weeks later, a new government was formed by Khomeini.

Your FRONTLINE Career

Is Being an NCS Agent for You?

Sounds Great
- Rescuing people in need of help
- Working with governments to keep people safe
- Coming up with creative ways to solve problems

Things to Think About
- Being willing to put one's own safety at risk to help others
- Having patience, since operations can take months to plan and carry out, and they may not go according to plan
- Keeping operations a secret and never telling anyone, even family, the details
- Willing to deceive others, such as border agents and government officials, to maintain cover

On November 4, 1979, a group of Khomeini's supporters raided the U.S. embassy in Iran. At the time, U.S. President Jimmy Carter had allowed the Shah to seek medical treatment in the United States. This angered Khomeini's supporters, who demanded that the U.S. send the Shah back to Iran to face justice. In order to force the U.S. to do this, the protesters took 66 Americans **hostage**. Six U.S. **diplomats** had escaped the raid and asked the Canadian embassy for help to flee Iran. The Americans, known as the Canadian Six, remained in hiding for months while the CIA and the Canadian government figured out an escape plan.

The CIA came up with a unique idea to help the Canadian Six leave Iran. CIA agents formed a fake movie production company called Studio Six Productions. They set up offices in an old Hollywood studio and wrote a script for a movie named *Argo*. Only a select few agents knew that the movie was not real. Then, the movie production team, which was made up of undercover CIA agents, made plans with the Iranian government to shoot the movie in Iran.

The day before they left Iran, the Canadian Six practiced their cover stories. They had to pretend that they were part of a movie production team. They were also given disguises and new clothes to make it look like they were from Hollywood.

CIA agents disguised as a movie crew traveled to Iran to look for places to film *Argo*. The Canadian Six then joined the film crew as it left Iran on January 27, 1980. They used fake Canadian passports to make their escape from the country. Soon after, the Canadian embassy in Iran closed, and the remaining Canadian diplomats flew back to Canada.

Studio Six Productions closed its doors, and *Argo* was never made. No one knew why until 1997, when the CIA revealed its role in the undercover operation known as the Canadian Caper. In 2012, actor Ben Affleck directed and starred in the movie *Argo*. It told the incredible story of the CIA undercover operation in Iran.

THE FBI

The FBI is the investigative arm of the U.S. Department of Justice (DoJ). It uses undercover operations to detect, prevent, and punish criminal activities that are a national security threat. These include crimes such as fraud, **public corruption**, terrorism, organized crime, **civil rights** violations, drug **trafficking**, and more. More than 35,000 people work for the FBI. They come from a variety of backgrounds and have a wide range of skills. They investigate crimes and enforce **federal** laws.

STRESSFUL WORK

Undercover FBI agents have a difficult job. They must work in crime rings and make criminals believe that they are one of them. Like actors, they play different roles. They may pretend to be killers for hire, burglars, gamblers, and international weapons dealers. Special agents are on the job 24 hours a day, 7 days a week, when working undercover. They can be sent to work in any of the FBI's 56 U.S. field offices at any time. Sometimes, they must work overseas for long periods of time.

An FBI mobile command center is equipped with communication tools to conduct operations in the field.

The FBI's Cyber Action Team (CAT) is made up of computer experts who can respond to cyber threats anywhere in the world within 48 hours.

GETTING INTO CHARACTER

To get into character, agents look for ways to relate to the criminals they are investigating. They try to find something to like about the person, so they can befriend them and gain their trust. The criminal might have a child, for instance, so agents might focus on the criminal's love for the child as a way to get them to open up to them.

SOLVING CYBERCRIMES

FBI agents try to prevent spies from obtaining top secret information and giving it to foreign governments. They also try to stop spies from stealing **trade secrets** from U.S. businesses and colleges. Spying often takes place online as data, or information, theft from computer networks. The FBI is the leading U.S. government cybercrime investigation agency. In 2012, it led an undercover operation called Operation Card Shop that stretched across four continents and led to 24 arrests in eight countries. The crimes involved hackers who would buy and sell credit card details, stolen identities, fake documents, and more. Operation Card Shop protected 400,000 potential victims and saved an estimated $205 million in losses. The **mission** lasted two years and involved some of the most wanted cybercriminals known for buying and selling stolen identities.

Tamer Elnoury:

TERROR PLOT RUINED

On April 22, 2013, an undercover FBI agent who uses the alias, or fake name, Tamer Elnoury helped stop what was supposed to be the largest terrorist attack on North American soil since September 11, 2001. The plot involved **al-Qaeda** supporters killing as many people as possible by derailing a train traveling from New York to Toronto.

Your FRONTLINE Career

Is Being an FBI Agent for You?

Sounds Great
• Working on high-profile cases
• Taking on a secret identity
• Helping prevent crimes and terror attacks, which could kill thousands of people

Things to Think About
• Being willing to live and work with terrorists and other criminals
• May be sent to work all over the world for any length of time
• Cannot take off weekends, evenings, or holidays to spend time with loved ones
• Keeping your identity a secret or risk being harmed

Elnoury was born in Egypt, but his family moved to the United States when he was a child. He spent 12 years investigating drug rings as an undercover police officer. The FBI then **recruited** him because he spoke Arabic. In 2012, the FBI assigned him to become friends with a suspected terrorist named Chiheb Esseghaier. Esseghaier was originally from Tunisia in Africa but was living in Montreal, Canada. The FBI had evidence that Esseghaier was working with al-Qaeda in Iran.

The FBI arranged for Elnoury to be on a flight that Esseghaier was taking. Elnoury then had to find a way to meet Esseghaier and become friends. Elnoury did this, and over the next 10 months, Elnoury and Esseghaier became very close. Esseghaier began to share details of his work with al-Qaeda. Eventually, Esseghaier recruited Elnoury to help him with his terror plot to derail the train. The FBI had enough information to arrest Esseghaier, but they decided to keep going with the investigation.

Esseghaier believed there was another man working with al-Qaeda in the United States. Elnoury kept working with Esseghaier to try to find out more about the man. However, on April 15, 2013, there was a terrorist attack at the Boston Marathon. Two bombs went off near the finish line of the race. The Canadian government wanted to stop any other potential attacks, and Esseghaier was a big threat. Esseghaier was arrested and eventually sentenced to life in prison based on the evidence Elnoury helped gather.

Elnoury has told his story many times, but he has never revealed his real name. He also wears a disguise when working with the media. Elnoury cannot risk blowing his cover since it would put his life in danger.

Brothers Tamerlan and Dzhokhar Tsarnaev, from Cambridge, Massachusetts, set off two bombs during the 2013 Boston Marathon. Three people were killed and hundreds of others were injured.

U.S. SPECIAL OPERATIONS FORCES

U.S. Special Operations Forces (SOF) are elite military units that perform complex missions in more than 140 countries. They are especially well equipped and receive more advanced training compared to other military units. Soldiers working in winter conditions may learn extreme skiing, for example. Others might receive training as scuba divers or skydivers to aid their missions. Most SOF missions are not known to the public. They involve high-risk situations, so it is important to keep a low profile for security reasons.

BEST OF THE BEST

It is very hard to become an SOF soldier. Typically, soldiers work for the military for about 10 years before gaining acceptance into the SOF. Most are in their mid-30s, have high levels of education, and have been **deployed** at least four times. In the past, female SOF members were not allowed to serve in combat roles. They have served as commanders, pilots, analysts, and other vital roles. But in 2016, the U.S. government allowed women to apply for **combat** positions for the first time.

*U.S. Air Force soldiers in SOF units learn basic winter warfare **tactics**, such as how to free fall from aircraft into the Arctic.*

WOMEN SPIES

*Canada's Special Forces are looking to recruit more women for **covert** operations. Special Forces need to have a more diverse team in order to conduct **intelligence**-gathering missions. For instance, on a mission, two men working together might seem out of place. However, a man and woman on the mission would more likely go unnoticed.*

Navy SEALs are trained to use a variety of weapons, including sniper rifles, combat knives, and automatic guns.

BUILT TOUGH

While each of the SOF are highly trained in special combat tactics, most focus on a specific type of mission. For example, the Navy SEALs are called in if underwater explosives need to be attached to an enemy ship. The Green Berets are the U.S. Army's SOF and are experts at sneaking behind enemy lines. They often **sabotage** enemy missions and convince rebel leaders to give up their fight. Delta Force is the most covert of all SOF units. It is sent in to help with secretive missions in situations where the U.S. military does not want anyone to know of its involvement.

Delta Force: FIGHTING ISIS

Islamic State of Iraq and Syria (ISIS) is a terrorist group that wants to set up a **fundamentalist** Islamic state in Iraq, Syria, and other parts of the Middle East. ISIS enforces a strict view of Islam. However, only a very small number of Muslims support ISIS. Members of this group use violence to support this vision. ISIS often destroys holy sites or attacks communities to gain attention. Members use social media to promote their cause and to recruit new members.

Your FRONTLINE Career

Is Being in the Delta Force for You?

Sounds Great
- Receiving highly specialized training to be part of an elite organization
- Working on a team with other top agents
- Taking part in top secret missions

Things to Think About
- Requires years of training and experience to join
- Must maintain a high level of physical fitness
- Must be willing to put your life at risk and be in difficult situations to complete a dangerous mission

In May 2015, President Barack Obama gave the order for about 24 members of the U.S. Army's Delta Force to conduct a top secret raid in Deir ez-Zor in eastern Syria.

A key ISIS leader known as Abu Sayyaf was killed during the raid. Typically, drones are used to attack ISIS targets. However, the U.S. government had been secretly watching Sayyaf for weeks and believed he had valuable information. They had tips from CIA informants, satellite imagery, drone **reconnaissance**, and electronic surveillance sources. They wanted to take Sayyaf alive, so that they could question him. They believed it was worth the risk to send in ground troops.

*Black Hawk helicopters operated by undercover forces have technology that makes them less detectable by **radar**. This makes it harder for the enemy to see them coming.*

Under cover of night, Delta Force flew into the area in Black Hawk helicopters and Osprey aircraft. ISIS attempted to defend their building from Delta Force but was unsuccessful. Delta Force took part in hand-to-hand combat with ISIS before blowing a hole in the side of the building where Sayyaf was staying. Inside, Delta Force encountered more ISIS fighters who used women and children as shields. Delta Force shot and killed the fighters without harming any innocent people.

Sayyaf was killed when he fought back. Delta Force captured Sayyaf's wife and held her for questioning. They also gained access to computers and other assets during the raid. Despite Sayyaf's death, Delta Force learned a lot about how ISIS operates, communicates, and earns money. Sayyaf was responsible for funding large portions of ISIS's operations. He had strong ties to an oil and gas company that gave money to support ISIS. About a dozen ISIS fighters were killed in the raid, but no members of Delta Force were harmed.

POLICE FORCE

Local police forces help keep communities safe by preventing and fighting against crime. One of the ways they do this is by conducting undercover operations. Local officers get involved with suspected criminals, living among them and pretending to be one of them as a way to collect information. Information about suspected criminals might include audio or video recordings, bank records, and eyewitness reports.

MASTERS OF DISGUISE

Where possible, officers try to dress and act in a similar fashion as they would in their real life. Some officers choose a name that is close to their own. That way, if they provide the wrong name, it is less likely to be noticed. Some police forces hire actors to give undercover officers tips about getting into their roles. They also provide training for any specific information officers may need to know, such as how to identify street drugs or use slang when they speak. Officers then spend weeks or even months building relationships with as many people in the crime ring as possible. They observe and investigate the actions of suspected criminals in the hope that they can gather enough information for an arrest.

When an undercover officer has enough evidence to prove that a suspect committed a crime, they ask the court to issue an arrest warrant. This is a piece of paper that gives permission to arrest a suspect.

RISKY BUSINESS

Undercover police officers who work near where they live with their families or where they grew up face a much higher risk of **exposure**. When possible, they are assigned to investigations that take place mainly in a part of the community where few people know them. This way, they are less likely to run into someone who could blow their cover. Sometimes, the undercover officer makes the arrest when the investigation is complete. At that time, officers reveal their true identity. This can be unsafe in some situations because other criminals might find out who the officer is and try to harm them.

TAKING ON AN OP

Most undercover officers have many years of experience working on a police force before they take on undercover assignments. Sometimes, new recruits or younger officers with less experience are asked to conduct an undercover investigation. If the case calls for someone to **infiltrate** a high school or a group of young people, the officers must be young to fit in.

Officers may need to blend in with teenagers or young adults in order to find out information about a crime.

Mr. Big:
CAPTURING A SUSPECT

Sometimes, police forces do not have enough evidence to convict suspects. They need the suspect to admit to their crime to guarantee a conviction. In the 1990s, Canada's Royal Canadian Mounted Police (RCMP) developed a tactic for getting suspects to confess to their crimes. Known as Mr. Big, the tactic has been used in hundreds of cases and is still in use today.

Your FRONTLINE Career

Is Being an Undercover Police Officer for You?

Sounds Great
• Working in a variety of settings, where each day is different
• Pretending to be a different person to do your job
• Helping put criminals in jail and keeping people safe
• Taking part in special training programs to learn new skills

Things to Think About
• Being away from friends and family for long periods of time
• Having to work with dangerous criminals and pretending to like them
• Being in danger after the investigation is complete

The first step in a Mr. Big operation is for undercover police officers to create a fake criminal organization. They pretend to be high-ranking members of the organization, and they find a way to get the suspect to join it. Over time, the undercover officers gain the suspect's trust and then ask the suspect to help with some criminal activities. For example, they might ask the suspect to deliver illegal goods, sell guns or drugs, or conduct a credit card scam. All of the crimes are fake and preplanned.

Sometimes, suspects are paid for their work. Other times, they are told that it is a test of their loyalty to the organization. As the undercover officers grow closer to the suspect, they encourage the person to share more details about their lives and their past. Eventually, they invite the suspect to meet the leader of the crime organization, or Mr. Big, as a show of trust. During these meetings, Mr. Big encourages suspects to openly talk about any crimes they may have committed. Mr. Big may even promise the suspect something in return for sharing the criminal history.

For example, he might say he has a connection in the police force who can cover up the crime, or he may offer to give the person a special role in the organization. In this way, Mr. Big gets the person to confess to a crime.

When carried out correctly, the Mr. Big tactic can prove highly useful. However, it comes with large risks. In many cases, the Supreme Court of Canada has not allowed confessions obtained using the Mr. Big tactic. This is because the confession is not given freely. The person is often offered a big benefit in return. Suspects might say they committed the crime just to get the reward, even if they did not do it. For this reason, Mr. Big is banned in some countries, such as the United States, United Kingdom, and Germany. But many cases in Canada would remain unsolved today had it not been for Mr. Big confessions.

Agents may be asked to transport drugs as part of their role in trying to catch and convict drug traffickers.

MISSIONS BEHIND THE FRONT LINE

Behind every undercover operation is a team of people who make the investigation possible. For people who do not want to work as undercover agents, law enforcement agencies offer plenty of other opportunities in a variety of fields. Important roles that work behind the scenes to support the teams on the front line include lab analysts, foreign policy advisers, engineers, forensic experts, scientists, technology specialists, and more. These roles are every bit as important as those of the people fighting out on the front line.

SCIENCE AND TECHNOLOGY SPECIALISTS

Law enforcement agencies rely heavily on computers and the Internet to research and analyze information. Information technology (IT) engineers help keep computer networks and databases up and running. They make sure that agents have access to e-mail, video conferencing, and other programs they need to securely communicate with team members and transfer files. They also ensure all data stored in computer systems is protected from cyber threats. Software engineers design and develop computer programs and surveillance tools to assist undercover agents with their day-to-day work.

IT specialists install computer hardware and software, test to ensure it works well, and troubleshoot any problems that may arise.

Intelligence analysts spend much of their time researching statistics, historical data, maps, and other information.

INTELLIGENCE ANALYSTS

Intelligence analysts collect information on security threats and crimes from a variety of sources. They analyze the details to determine if the threat is real. Most analysts focus on a specific field of study. They are assigned to a case and must then find as much information as possible relating to their area of expertise. They might gather evidence in the field, research online, review data and statistics, speak with witnesses or other experts, or conduct searches. Analysts sift through the information for the most important details. They use critical thinking skills to make judgments and recommendations about how to handle certain threats or crimes. Then, they document their findings in a report for other members of the agency, such as undercover officers, who decide the next steps.

LEARN THE LANGUAGE

Both the CIA and the FBI place a high importance on foreign languages. They hire foreign language instructors to teach new languages to undercover agents. They also employ people who can read, write, and speak at least one foreign language fluently. These people help translate and analyze information relating to crimes.

Monique Brillhart:

FBI FORENSICS

Forensic science is an important part of any criminal investigation. It produces clear facts that undercover agents can use to connect suspects with specific crimes. Forensic scientists apply the newest technologies to analyze and interpret evidence. Some forensic scientists work in labs, using microscopes and other tools to examine physical evidence such as documents and fibers from clothes. They analyze drugs, blood, and other fluids. Forensic scientists write reports that outline their findings. They are sometimes asked to **testify** in court because scientific facts cannot be disputed.

Your FRONTLINE Career

Is Being a forensic Scientist for You?

Sounds Great

- Working in one of the world's largest crime labs
- Using science to help solve crimes
- Learning the latest scientific methods and techniques
- Looking for evidence at crime scenes and examining the evidence to solve crimes

Things to Think About

- Paying strong attention to detail is vital
- Being very careful so as not to damage evidence
- Believing in your ability and being willing to testify in court

Many law enforcement agencies rely on forensic scientists, such as Monique Brillhart, to help solve crimes. Brillhart works as a **latent print** examiner for the FBI. She collects and analyzes fingerprints and then compares them to a suspect's prints, or she looks for matches in a computer database of prints. Brillhart studied biology in college, and she also took courses in forensic science. She knew she wanted to work as a forensic scientist but had trouble finding a job in that field, so she worked in a variety of jobs before going back to school.

While working on her master's degree at Johns Hopkins University, Brillhart saw an ad for the FBI. It was her dream job. Months later, she got the job. Now, Brillhart spends most days analyzing prints.

Forensic scientists cover objects with fluorescent powders or sprays. Then, they hold an ultraviolet light over the objects to reveal any fingerprints.

She works on the Latent Print Operations Unit (LPOU) and is the coordinator of the Hazardous Evidence Analysis Team (HEAT). As part of HEAT, she looks for latent prints on evidence that has been contaminated with hazardous chemical, **biological**, **radiological**, or nuclear materials.

Brillhart has other duties, too. She processes evidence and testifies in court as an expert witness. She also works with **humanitarian** organizations to identify disaster victims. Brillhart trains new latent print examiners when they join the FBI. She even teaches fingerprint analysis skills to law enforcement workers in other countries.

COULD YOU BE ON THE FRONT LINE?

Do you have what it takes to work as an undercover agent? Here are some of the key things to think about if you want a career in undercover operations.

EDUCATION

Most law enforcement agencies require a high school diploma or GED. The majority of undercover agents also have a college degree. Undercover agents often specialize in a certain field, such as computer science or forensic science. Courses in law enforcement or criminal justice are also useful. Most agencies have their own special training programs. These might include foreign languages, firearms, first aid, and self-defense courses.

FAMILY

Working undercover means spending long periods of time out of contact with friends and family. Agents typically adopt a new identity, which includes living away from home for weeks, months, or even years. Some agents are required to live in foreign countries. Would you be happy being away from your family? Talk to your family about the impact your absence might have on them.

FITNESS

Having strong mental health helps agents cope with stressful situations. Physical fitness is also important. Agents must pass hearing and vision tests. They must also pass strength tests that include timed sprints and doing as many sit-ups and push-ups as possible in a certain period of time. Eating a balanced diet and exercising regularly will help you prepare to become an undercover agent.

DISCIPLINE

Undercover agents are expected to uphold the highest levels of the law. Potential agents often go through a series of interviews and background checks to show they are upstanding citizens and do not have a criminal past.

QUALITIES

Undercover agents need to have very good communication skills. They need to speak with many people to collect facts and then write down information to share with others. They should be open to different points of view and have a desire to help others. Strong decision-making skills are also important. Agents often need to solve problems quickly and make complex choices with little time to think.

DEDICATION AND COMMITMENT

Working undercover is hard, risky work. Agents work long hours, including evenings and weekends. They need to be on call all hours of the day or night. Once an agent agrees to play a role in an investigation, he or she cannot stop. Agents must commit to seeing it through without blowing their cover. Undercover work can put a lot of stress on an agent's physical and mental health.

CARVING A CAREER

There are many different undercover opportunities in U.S. and Canadian law enforcement agencies. Find out about them, and think about what you might like to do.

GLOSSARY

al-Qaeda A militant Muslim group that wants to remove all Western influence from Arab nations

biological Describes germ warfare, which is a system of using dangerous and deadly bacteria and viruses to attack civilians

Central Intelligence Agency (CIA) The U.S. government agency that gathers, processes, and analyzes national security information

civil rights A set of rights that are designed to protect people from unfair treatment and to ensure everyone receives equal treatment

combat Fighting between two or more groups of armed forces

cover A fake identity or disguise used to hide and protect a person's true identity

covert Secret or hidden

culture The religion, art, and way of life of a people or country

deployed Sent on a mission or tour of duty

diplomats People appointed by a government to work with other governments

evidence A collection of facts and information that help prove if something is true or false

exiled Forced to live away from one's home

exposure The act of uncovering a person's true identity

federal Relating to the central government of a country

Federal Bureau of Investigation (FBI) The intelligence and security service of the United States that works within the country

fundamentalist A person who believes in the strict interpretation of their religion's writings and teachings

hostage Someone held captive by another

humanitarian Describes a person or organization that works to improve the welfare of people

identity The looks, beliefs, and personality that make up who a person is

infiltrate To secretly gain access to an organization or place in order to find information

informants People who provide information to another person or organization

intelligence Secret information

investigation The act of carefully searching and examining a person or situation

latent print A fingerprint that cannot be seen by the naked eye

law enforcement agencies Organizations that are responsible for enforcing the law

mission An important task carried out on behalf of an organization

National Clandestine Service (NCS) The undercover arm of the CIA

nuclear Related to weapons that use deadly and destructive nuclear energy

organized crime rings Groups of criminals who work together to commit crimes

public corruption When a government worker does a favor for someone in exchange for something of value, such as being paid to vote in a certain way

radar A machine that can pick up the position of a person or object using radio waves

radiological Related to deadly nuclear radiation

reconnaissance A survey to secretly find out about enemy territory

recruited Signed up or employed

sabotage To destroy something on purpose

secret service agencies Government departments that use agents to work undercover or in secret to gather information

security threats People or objects that pose a danger or risk of harm

tactics Plans or ways to achieve a specific goal

terrorist A person or group that uses illegal fighting and violence, especially against civilians, to gain political or religious aims

testify To make a statement in a court of law

trade secrets Secret techniques used by businesses to create their products

trafficking Trading, usually in something illegal

LEARNING MORE

Discover more about undercover operations and careers on the front line.

BOOKS

Boudreau, Helene. *Crimebusting and Detection*. Crabtree Publishing Company, 2009.

Briggs, Andy. *How to Be an International Spy: Your Training Manual, Should You Choose to Accept It.* Lonely Planet Kids, 2015.

Doeden, Matt. *Can You Survive in the Special Forces?: An Interactive Survival Adventure* (You Choose: Survival). Capstone Press, 2012.

Mara, Wil. *FBI Special Agent* (21st Century Skills Library: Cool STEAM Careers). Cherry Lake Publishing, 2015.

WEBSITES

To work for the CSIS, you must be a Canadian citizen, have a driver's license, and be willing to live anywhere in Canada. For more information, visit:
www.canada.ca/en/security-intelligence-service/corporate/csis-jobs.html

To join the CIA, you need to be a U.S. citizen and must be at least 18 years old. Find out more at:
www.cia.gov/careers

To learn more about the wide range of careers with the FBI, visit:
www.fbijobs.gov

Find out which U.S. Special Operations Forces is right for you at:
www.military.com/military-fitness/fitness-test-prep/which-specops-is-right-for-me

Learn all about how to become a member of the RCMP at:
www.rcmp-grc.gc.ca/en/careers

INDEX

A
Affleck, Ben 11
al-Qaeda 14, 15
Argo 10, 11

B
Boston Marathon bombing 15
Brillhart, Monique 26–27

C
Canadian Security Intelligence
 Service (CSIS) 8
Canadian Six 10–11
Central Intelligence Agency (CIA)
 8–9, 10–11, 18, 25
civil rights 12
combat 16, 17, 19
Cyber Action Team (CAT) 13
cybercrimes 5, 13

D
Delta Force 17, 18–19
diplomats 10, 11
drugs 5, 6, 12, 14, 20, 22, 23, 26

E
electronic surveillance 8, 12, 19
Elnoury, Tamer 14–15
evidence 4, 6, 14, 15, 20, 22,
 25, 26, 27

F
FBI mobile command center 12
Federal Bureau of Investigation
 (FBI) 5, 12–13, 14–15, 25,
 26–27

G
Gambino crime family 5
Garcia, Jack 5
Green Berets 17

H
hackers 5
Hazardous Evidence Analysis
 Team (HEAT) 27

I
informants 8, 9, 18
intelligence 7, 17
Iranian Revolution 10, 11
ISIS 18, 19

K
Khomeini, Ayatollah 10, 11

L
languages 9, 25
Latent Print Operations Unit
 (LPOU) 27

M
Mr. Big operation 22–23

N
National Clandestine Service
 (NCS) 8
Navy SEALs 17

O
Obama, President Barack 18
Operation Card Shop 13
organized crime 5, 12, 20

P
public corruption 12

R
radar 19
Royal Canadian Mounted Police
 (RCMP) 22, 23

S
security threats 8, 14, 15, 25
Special Operations Forces (SOF)
 16–17, 18–19

T
trafficking 12, 23

U
U.S. Air Force 17

ABOUT THE AUTHOR

Heather C. Hudak has written hundreds of educational books on all kinds of topics. When she's not writing, Heather enjoys traveling the world or camping in the mountains near her home with her husband and many rescue pets. In researching this book, Heather discovered she would love to work as an undercover agent to collect top secret information from foreign governments.